HARD AS NAILS

Travelers and Explorers

TRACEY TURNER

ILLUSTRATED BY JAMIE LENMAN

Crabtree Publishing Company

www.crabtreebooks.com

Crabtree Publishing Company
www.crabtreebooks.com
1-800-387-7650

616 Welland Ave.
St. Catharines, ON
L2M 5V6

PMB 59051, 350 Fifth Ave.
59th Floor,
New York, NY

Published by Crabtree Publishing Company in 2016.

Author: Tracey Turner

Illustrator: Jamie Lenman

Project coordinator: Kelly Spence

Editor: Becca Sjonger

Proofreader: Wendy Scavuzzo

Prepress technician: Tammy McGarr

Print coordinator: Margaret Amy Salter

Copyright © 2015 A & C Black

Text copyright © 2015 Tracey Turner

Illustrations copyright © 2015 Jamie Lenman

Additional illustrations © Shutterstock

Printed in the USA / 082015 / SN20150529

First published 2015 by A & C Black, an imprint of Bloomsbury Publishing Plc.

Library and Archives Canada Cataloguing in Publication

Turner, Tracey, author
        Hard as nails travelers and explorers / Tracey Turner ; Jamie Lenman, illustrator.

(Hard as nails in history)
Includes index.
ISBN 978-0-7787-1521-4 (bound).--
ISBN 978-0-7787-1525-2 (paperback)

    1. Explorers--Biography--Juvenile literature. 2. Explorers--Juvenile literature. 3. Adventure and adventurers--Juvenile literature. 4. Voyages and travels--Juvenile literature. 5. Discoveries in geography--Juvenile literature. I. Lenman, Jamie, illustrator II. Title.

G200.T87 2015   j910.92′2   C2015-903046-3

Library of Congress Cataloging-in-Publication Data

CIP available at Library of Congress

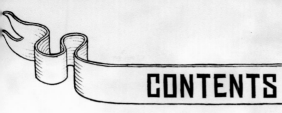

CONTENTS

INTRODUCTION

This book contains the toughest and most courageous explorers and travelers in the history of the world. Some of them navigated uncharted waters, some braved the icy landscapes of the freezing poles, and one even set foot on the surface of the Moon.

FIND OUT ABOUT . . .

- The mysterious source of the White Nile

- The court of Kublai Khan

- The search for the Fountain of Youth

- The awful fates of many explorers

If you've ever wanted to cross the Rocky Mountains, explore an Aztec city, or travel the Northwest Passage, read on. Journey through crocodile-infested swamps, across wind-blown wastelands, and into the vast emptiness of space.

As well as learning about stories of discovery and courage, you might be in for a few surprises. For example, did you know that Walter Raleigh searched for a city made of gold? Or that Captain Cook was chopped to pieces?

You're about to meet some of the bravest and most fearless explorers who ever lived . . .

Plus turn to pages 32 and 33 to learn all about disgusting and deadly diseases explorers encountered!

ROALD AMUNDSEN

Roald Amundsen was one of the toughest adventurers of all time. He became the greatest polar explorer ever.

A CHILLY EXPEDITION

Amundsen was born in 1872 in Norway. As soon as he was old enough, he joined an expedition to the Antarctic. The ship he sailed on became trapped in the ice and was stuck for over a year. Almost everyone got scurvy, a disease caused by a lack of vitamin C. Amundsen, a tough young man, took charge. He organized people to catch penguins and seals for food, and to turn the animals' skins into clothing and blankets. Eventually spring arrived and the ice melted—a little—and the expedition became the first ever to survive a whole winter in the Antarctic.

THE NORTHWEST PASSAGE

Amundsen wasn't discouraged by his icy experience. In 1903, he set off on his own expedition to find the Northwest Passage—a waterway connecting the Atlantic and Pacific that explorers had been seeking for hundreds of years. When he arrived in the Arctic, the native people who lived there taught Amundsen about igloos and sled-pulling dog teams. By 1906, he had become the first person to navigate the Northwest Passage.

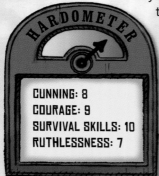

HARDOMETER

CUNNING: 8
COURAGE: 9
SURVIVAL SKILLS: 10
RUTHLESSNESS: 7

ANTARCTIC EXPEDITION

In 1911, Amundsen was back in the Antarctic, determined to reach the South Pole before Robert Scott's expedition did (see page 52). He had four companions, four sleds, and 52 dogs. He used his polar survival skills to combat the coldest temperatures on Earth, icy blizzards, and perilous crevasses. Amundsen reached the South Pole on December 14, 1911, a month before Scott. By that time, the team had eaten most of the dogs. Amundsen returned to Norway a hero, and was awarded a gold medal by the National Geographic Society in the United States.

POLE POSITION

Amundsen never stopped exploring. By the time he died in a plane crash in 1928, he had become the first person to visit both poles on foot and by air.

CHRISTOPHER COLUMBUS

Christopher Columbus discovered the New World—even though he wasn't really looking for it.

HOIST THE SAILS!

Christopher Columbus was born in Italy in 1451. He went to sea when he was 14. Columbus settled in Portugal, the seafaring capital of the world at the time. He wanted to find a new sea route to Asia, which he hoped would make him rich and be an adventure at the same time. Columbus came up with the new and exciting idea of getting there by sailing west (like most educated people of the time, he knew the world was round).

I'VE FOUND INDIA!

LAND HO!

Columbus needed money and ships for his voyage. No one in Portugal would help him, but King Ferdinand and Queen Isabella of Spain liked his ideas. They gave him the money to fund his expedition. In 1492, Columbus set sail in three ships, and by October he reached the Caribbean. He thought he had reached the Indies (now called Asia), so he called the locals "Indians." Columbus traveled on to Cuba and Hispaniola (modern-day Haiti and the Dominican Republic), where he built a fort from the wreck of one of the ships and left some of his men. Then he sailed back to Spain with his ships full of exotic plants, gold, parrots, and a few of the local people. Columbus announced that he had discovered the West Indies.

ROUGH SEAS

Columbus sailed on two more voyages, and explored the Caribbean coast of South America. On the second of the two voyages, he got into trouble. The people who had been left at the fort on Hispaniola had been killed by the locals, and Columbus was accused of managing things badly. He had also made the mistake of not finding any gold. Columbus returned to Spain as a prisoner on one of his own ships.

FINAL VOYAGE

Columbus persuaded the Spanish to send him on his final Atlantic voyage in 1504. His ships were wrecked on the Jamaican coast and he had to be rescued. A year and a half later, he died, without ever knowing that he hadn't sailed to Asia after all. Columbus's discovery of the New World changed history.

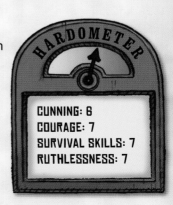

HARDOMETER

CUNNING: 6
COURAGE: 7
SURVIVAL SKILLS: 7
RUTHLESSNESS: 7

THE NEW WORLD

More explorers followed Christopher Columbus across the Atlantic Ocean from Europe. In the 1500s, the known world consisted of Europe, Africa, and Asia—the Old World. Now explorers traveled to North and South America—the New World.

INVADING THE NEW WORLD

People living in the New World were in for a big surprise, and it wasn't a nice one. When Europeans arrived, they claimed land for their own countries without bothering to ask if it already belonged to anyone. Columbus enslaved many native peoples. Hundreds of thousands of them became slaves, were killed in battles with the Europeans, or died from diseases brought across the ocean. The native peoples of some parts of the New World died out completely. It has been estimated that around one hundred million people died.

RICH EUROPEANS

Once they had established power over the people who lived in the New World, the European invaders began making themselves rich by exploiting the land's rich resources. Gold, silver, and other precious metals were found in South America. Vast expanses of fertile land could be used to grow crops such as sugar, which fed the Europeans' growing appetite for sweet treats. More and more Europeans left their own crowded countries to settle in the New World.

NEW WORLD FOOD

Chocolate, made from the beans of the cacao tree native to Central and South America, was made into a bitter drink by the Aztecs. A sweetened version became fashionable all over Europe, although solid chocolate wasn't eaten until the 1800s. The Old World also got its first taste of tomatoes, sweet corn, turkey, vanilla, pineapples, and potatoes from the New World.

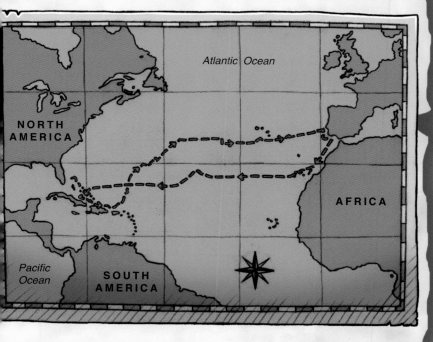

This map shows the first route Christopher Columbus took to the New World. This trip was followed by three more voyages.

AMELIA EARHART

Defying the conventions of her time, Amelia Earhart was a pioneering aviator. She became the first woman to fly solo across the Atlantic and Pacific oceans.

FIRST FLIGHT

Amelia Earhart worked as a nurse and a social worker before she first flew in a plane in 1920. The flight appealed to the 23-year-old woman's sense of adventure, and within a week she was taking flying lessons. Six months later, she had saved up enough money to buy her first plane. She flew the bright yellow plane, nicknamed "The Canary," to a height of 14,000 feet (4,267 m), setting her first women's world record.

ATLANTIC FLIGHT

The race was on to be the first female pilot to cross the Atlantic. Earhart did it in 1928, flying with two male pilots from Newfoundland to Wales in a journey that took 21 hours. Flying in the 1920s was much more dangerous than it is today. Three women had already died in 1928 while attempting to set the record.

HARDOMETER

CUNNING: 7
COURAGE: 10
SURVIVAL SKILLS: 6
RUTHLESSNESS: 5

GOING SOLO

Earhart planned her next daring expedition: a solo flight across the Atlantic Ocean. She took off from Newfoundland in 1932 on a flight plagued by strong winds, freezing temperatures, and mechanical problems. She was heading for Paris, but made an emergency landing in a field in Ireland. For making it across the Atlantic, Earhart was awarded a Distinguished Flying Cross—the first ever given to a woman. She said the flight proved men and women were equal in "intelligence, coordination, speed, coolness, and willpower." In 1935, Earhart became the first woman to fly solo across the Pacific Ocean from Honolulu, Hawaii, to California.

AROUND THE WORLD

Earhart wanted to become the first woman to fly around the world—a journey of over 28,950 miles (46,600 km). She left from Florida in 1937. In less than a month, she and her co-pilot Fred Noonan had covered over 22,000 miles (35,406 km). For the final leg of the journey, from New Guinea to Howland Island in the middle of the Pacific, they threw anything that wasn't absolutely necessary out of the plane to make room for extra fuel. But they never reached their destination. No one knows what happened, but Earhart and Noonan probably ran out of fuel and died at sea.

FEMALE EXPLORERS

As well as having to contend with shark-infested seas, angry leopards, and Pacific high winds, women explorers have had to battle against the conventions of society. In the past, they were expected to take care of their homes while also looking after their children and husbands. And that was just the rich women—poor women had even fewer options. Here are three more truly tough women, who defied convention to become explorers.

ISABELLE EBERHARDT

Eberhardt was born in Switzerland in 1877. She first traveled to North Africa at age 20 with her mother. After both her parents died, Isabelle spent most of the rest of her life in Africa. She often dressed as a man to get around the strict rules for women, and did her best to help the poor and fight injustice. She sometimes got into trouble. In 1901, a man attacked her with a sword and almost cut off her arm. Eberhardt forgave him and pleaded for his life when he was sentenced to death (she succeeded). Her life was cut short when she died in a flash flood in Algeria in 1904.

ISABELLA BIRD

Born in England in 1831, Isabella Bird was 41 before she finally achieved her exploring ambitions. But she made up for lost time by visiting Australia, Hawaii (where she climbed volcanoes), and the Rocky Mountains, which she explored in the company of a notorious outlaw. She made other expeditions to Japan, Vietnam, Singapore, Malaysia, India, Turkey, Kurdistan, Iran, and finally China. She was planning a return trip to China when she died at age 72.

ALEXANDRINE TINNÉ

Alexandrine Tinné was born in 1835 in the Netherlands. After her rich father died when she was ten, Tinné and her mother used their great wealth to travel around Europe, the Middle East, and Egypt. They explored the course of the White Nile River in the Sudan. They were hoping to explore the lakes of central Africa when both Tinné's mother and aunt died of fever. Tinné decided to keep exploring. She was crossing the Sahara Desert in the company of Tuareg nomads in 1869 when she was murdered—possibly because her water tanks were rumored to be filled with gold.

ISABELLA BIRD

BURKE AND WILLS

HARD AS NAILS RATING: 6.3

Robert Burke and William Wills led an expedition across Australia, but they never made it home.

A BAD BEGINNING

Robert Burke, a police superintendent with no exploring experience, was appointed to lead an expedition across the unexplored middle of Australia from north to south. William Wills was Burke's second-in-command. In August 1860, they left from Melbourne with a team of 22 men, plus horses, camels, and wagons. It took them two months to reach Menindee, although the mail coach regularly made the journey in just over a week. Burke knew that there was a reward for the first north-south trip, and he knew there was a rival expedition, so he and Wills went ahead with a smaller group, desperate to win.

SWAMPLAND

At Cooper Creek in Queensland, the group split again. Burke carried on with Wills and two other men, Charles Gray and John King, in the sizzling heat of the Australian summer, leaving the others to wait. Sick and exhausted, the small group staggered on. Burke and Wills traveled the final 15 miles (24 km) on their own and came within sight of the northern coast of Australia. They didn't quite make it all the way because of crocodile-infested swamps. The two men met up with Gray and King, and began

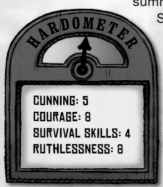

HARDOMETER

CUNNING: 5
COURAGE: 8
SURVIVAL SKILLS: 4
RUTHLESSNESS: 8

the rain-soaked journey back to Cooper Creek and the rest of the team. They were tired, sick, and low on supplies, so they ate their exhausted animals, plus a large snake discovered by Gray.

A HOPELESS JOURNEY

Gray died, and when the remaining three men arrived at Cooper Creek they discovered that everyone else had left only hours before. Burke set out for the appropriately named Mount Hopeless, but returned to Cooper Creek when the last two camels died. The three men were on their way to an Aboriginal camp to ask for help when Burke and Wills both died. The only survivor of their small team was John King, who was helped by the Aboriginal people. Burke and Wills did become the first non-Aboriginal people to cross the continent, but they didn't live to receive the prize money.

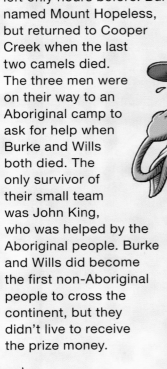

CAPTAIN COOK

**HARD AS NAILS
RATING: 8.3**

**Captain James Cook
discovered and named
hundreds of islands and coasts,
sailed all the world's oceans,
and traveled around the world—twice!**

UNCHARTED TERRITORY

James Cook was a lieutenant in the British Royal Navy.
As a skilled and experienced sailor, he was chosen to
captain a voyage to the Pacific in 1768. His crew included
astronomers to observe the planets, and botanists to
record and collect samples of the plants and animals
they found. After a stay in Tahiti, Cook searched for the
fabled but unmapped "southern continent." He found New
Zealand instead, and mapped both the North and South
Islands of the country. He sailed west to the east coast
of Australia, which he mapped and promptly claimed for
Britain, naming it New South Wales. He returned from the
voyage having mapped 4,970 miles (8,000 km) of previously
uncharted territory.

THE SOUTHERN CONTINENT

HARDOMETER

CUNNING: 8
COURAGE: 9
SURVIVAL SKILLS: 8
RUTHLESSNESS: 8

Cook had been so successful on his
first trip that he was soon off again.
In 1772, he sailed with two ships
determined to find the southern
continent he had searched for
on his first voyage. In 1773, he
came closer to the South Pole
than anyone before him—he just
missed Antarctica.

THE NORTHWEST PASSAGE

By this time, Cook was famous and he could have retired, but he couldn't resist the quest for the Northwest Passage (a shortcut linking the Atlantic and Pacific oceans). He didn't find it. Instead he spent six months mapping the northwest coast of North America, and discovering the Hawaiian Islands. He got along with the Hawaiians at first, but things soon took a turn for the worse.

COOK'S HORRIBLE END

Cook outstayed his welcome with the Hawaiians. He was attacked and killed by them, along with ten of his men. The bodies were cut up and shared among the Hawaiian chiefs. The crew asked for Cook's body to be returned to them, and finally gruesome packages began to arrive—pieces of burnt bones with some flesh left on them, and various body parts. In the end, Cook's remains were buried at sea.

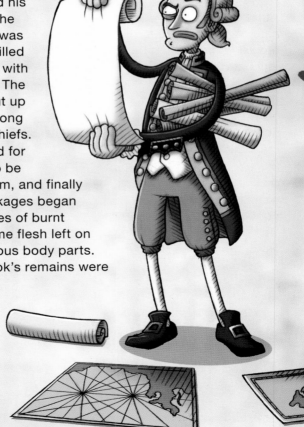

EXPLORING AUSTRALIA

Dutch explorer Willem Janszoon was the first European to land in Australia after crossing the ocean from the islands of Indonesia in 1606. Captain Cook (see page 20) was the first to explore the east coast of Australia in 1770. Not long after, the British began to colonize the huge Australian continent.

HARD AS NAILS EXPLORERS

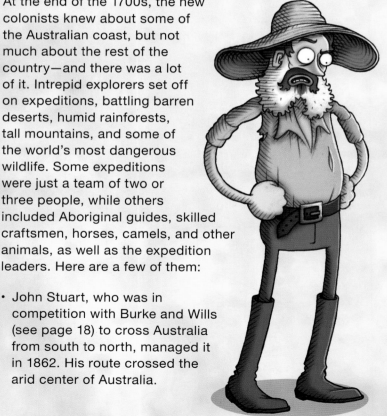

EDWARD EYRE

At the end of the 1700s, the new colonists knew about some of the Australian coast, but not much about the rest of the country—and there was a lot of it. Intrepid explorers set off on expeditions, battling barren deserts, humid rainforests, tall mountains, and some of the world's most dangerous wildlife. Some expeditions were just a team of two or three people, while others included Aboriginal guides, skilled craftsmen, horses, camels, and other animals, as well as the expedition leaders. Here are a few of them:

- John Stuart, who was in competition with Burke and Wills (see page 18) to cross Australia from south to north, managed it in 1862. His route crossed the arid center of Australia.

- Edward Eyre and his Aboriginal friend Wylie were part of a team that crossed southern Australia from west to east, a journey that took them across the hot, dry Nullarbor Plain. Their expedition quickly became a desperate search for water. Aboriginal people taught them to suck on gumtree roots and where to dig for water.

- Ludwig Leichhardt traveled from Sydney, on the east coast, to Port Essington, near Darwin in the north of Australia. It was 3,100 miles (4,988 km) of perilous country, which he covered in 18 months. Two years later, he set off on an attempt to travel from Brisbane in the east to Perth in the west, across the center of Australia. Leichhardt and his team disappeared. No trace of them has ever been found.

ABORIGINAL AUSTRALIANS

Aboriginal people had been living in Australia for thousands of years before the European colonists arrived. Many Aboriginal people died from diseases brought to Australia by Europeans, especially smallpox and tuberculosis. Their land was taken from them, and they weren't given the same rights as the settlers.

WYLIE

HERNÁN CORTÉS

Cortés was a Spanish conquistador who crossed the Atlantic to conquer the Aztecs of Central America.

ADVENTURES IN THE NEW WORLD

Hernán Cortés studied law at university, but he gave it up for a life of adventure. In 1504, he sailed for the island of Hispaniola (now Haiti and the Dominican Republic), then to Cuba. While in Cuba, he helped conqueror Diego Velázquez gain control of the island. Cortés earned a reputation for ruthlessness and courage in the process. In 1518, he took charge of an expedition to Mexico, which had only recently been discovered by Europeans.

AZTEC EMPEROR

When Cortés got to Mexico, his men didn't want to stay. So, in true tough-guy style, he sank the ships they had arrived in—now the conquest had to succeed! Cortés headed for the beautiful capital city of the mighty Aztec empire, Tenochtitlan. He was welcomed by the Aztec emperor, Montezuma II, who thought Cortés was the god Quetzalcoatl. Cortés imprisoned Montezuma and demanded a huge ransom for his release.

HARDOMETER

CUNNING: 8
COURAGE: 9
SURVIVAL SKILLS: 8
RUTHLESSNESS: 10

REVOLTING AZTECS

Jealous of Cortés, Velázquez sailed to Mexico ready to fight. Cortés left Tenochtitlan to deal with Velázquez. While he was away, there was an Aztec revolt. When Cortés returned, he learned Montezuma had been killed in the mayhem, and the Spanish had been driven out of the city by angry Aztecs. Cortés besieged Tenochtitlan for three months, starving the Aztecs to death. When the city fell, Cortés destroyed it and built Mexico City on its ruins. He showed no mercy to the Aztecs and other native peoples. Many of them were killed, or they died from diseases the Europeans brought with them.

EXPLORING CALIFORNIA

Cortés was made governor of the old Aztec empire. But the Spanish thought he was getting too powerful, so they sent him back to Spain and reduced his powers. Cortés returned to Central America and carried on exploring, hoping to find a sea route between the Atlantic and the Pacific oceans. He was disappointed, but he cheered up when he discovered California instead. He finally returned to Spain in 1541, where he died six years later.

BURTON AND SPEKE

**HARD AS NAILS
RATING: 7.3**

**Victorian explorers Richard Burton
and John Speke searched for the
source of the Nile in Africa,
but only one of them found it.**

THE SOURCE OF THE NILE

The Blue Nile joins the White Nile to form the Nile River
that flows through Egypt. The Blue Nile's source had been
discovered in the mountains of Ethiopia, but the source of
the White Nile was a mystery. English explorers Richard
Burton and John Speke set off in 1857 to discover the
mysterious source.

TERRIBLE EXPLORERS

Burton had injured his legs, Speke had an eye problem
and an ear infection, and both men were suffering from
malaria, so they had to be carried by porters. Speke's ear
infection was especially gross: a beetle had crawled into his
ear one night and he had tried to kill it with a small knife,
badly damaging his ear. Despite all this, Burton and Speke
became the first Europeans to explore Lake Tanganyika.
Burton was too sick to continue, but Speke went on
without him to look for a great lake that some traders had
described. Farther north he found it, and renamed it Lake
Victoria after the British queen.

BURTON GETS ANGRY

Burton was furious that Speke had discovered the lake
without him—especially if it was the source of the White Nile
as Speke claimed. The men had an enormous fight. Speke
returned to England ahead of Burton, claimed all the credit,
and made the expedition famous. Burton was outraged,

especially when Speke was sent back to Lake Victoria on his own. When Speke returned, he said that Lake Victoria definitely was the source of the White Nile, but he hadn't done much to prove it. Burton said Speke didn't know what he was talking about.

A HEATED DEBATE

In 1864, the two men were due to have a public debate about the source of the White Nile. But the day before the debate, Speke shot and killed himself while he was hunting. No one's sure whether he had meant to kill himself. Although he hadn't proven it, Speke was right about Lake Victoria: Henry Stanley confirmed it was the source of the White Nile a few years later.

HARDOMETER

CUNNING: 7
COURAGE: 8
SURVIVAL SKILLS: 6
RUTHLESSNESS: 8

LEIF ERIKSSON

Nearly 500 years before Columbus, Viking Leif Eriksson had already sailed across the Atlantic to North America.

WESTERN LAND

Eriksson was born around 970 CE in Iceland. He moved to Greenland after his father, Erik the Red, was exiled. In Greenland, Eriksson heard the story of an Icelandic trader called Bjarni Herjólfsson, who said he had been blown off course between Iceland and Greenland, and had spotted land to the west full of thick forests and green hills. Eriksson was ready for adventure, and he planned his own expedition.

LEIF SETS SAIL

Around the year 1000, Eriksson sailed his Viking longship with a crew of 35 in search of the new land. He didn't have a map, or even a compass, but he followed Herjólfsson's description as best he could. He stopped in places he called Helluland (probably Baffin Island) and Markland (probably Labrador). Battling through howling winds, fierce currents, and navigating around icebergs, Eriksson was determined to keep sailing until he found the land of forests Herjólfsson had seen. The sailors rowed the Viking ship for days on end, living on porridge, dried fish, and meat.

HARDOMETER

CUNNING: 8
COURAGE: 9
SURVIVAL SKILLS: 9
RUTHLESSNESS: 8

VIKING VINLAND

Eventually, Eriksson did find the new western land. He landed in Newfoundland, a large island off the coast of Canada, and called it Vinland. Eriksson and his crew built houses along the mouth of a river and stayed for the winter. In the 1960s, an archaeological dig in northern Newfoundland discovered a Viking settlement that fit the description of Vinland. (The ancient settlement is now named L'Anse aux Meadows.)

RETURN TO VINLAND

Leif returned to Greenland with stories of trees (which were in short supply in Iceland and Greenland), fruits, and rivers teeming with fish. A group of a hundred or so Greenlanders left for the new land, but the native people who lived there didn't make them very welcome, so they came back. Even though he didn't stay, Leif Eriksson is famous as the first European ever to set foot on North American soil.

LEWIS AND CLARK

HARD AS NAILS
RATING: 7.8

**Meriwether Lewis and William Clark
became the first Americans to travel
across the vast North American continent.**

MOUNTAINS AND MAMMOTHS

In 1803, President Thomas Jefferson sent
Lewis and Clark to find a route along the Missouri River
and over the Rocky Mountains to the Pacific Ocean.
Their mission was to explore the uncharted west, lay claim
to land, and establish trade with the native peoples along
the way. Jefferson thought they would find volcanoes,
woolly mammoths, and mountains of salt.

FROZEN RIVER

Lewis, Clark, and their team set off in three boats from St. Louis in the midwestern United States. The Missouri River took them north into what is now North Dakota, where they spent their first winter because the river was frozen solid. They hired a French-Canadian fur trapper and his wife Sacagawea. She was from the Shoshone nation and turned out to be very helpful. Sacagawea helped with the explorers' route and negotiations with native peoples, found edible plants, and made clothes and shoes. One chief they met turned out to be her long-lost brother!

BEARS AND BLIZZARDS

When the ice melted in spring, the explorers entered territory where no settler had ever set foot. Their journey took them across the Rocky Mountains, over the Great Falls, through sandstorms and blizzards, all the way to the Pacific Ocean. On the way, they encountered grizzly bears and different native tribes—some were friendly but others weren't.

TRIUMPHANT RETURN

On the way back, Lewis and Clark split up for part of the journey. When they met again, one of Clark's team mistook Lewis for an elk and shot him through the thigh. But Lewis was tough enough to limp back to St. Louis. The pair became the first non-native people to cross the huge continent of North America, arriving two years, four months, and ten days after they had left. Everyone had presumed they were dead. Lewis and Clark were welcomed home as heroes.

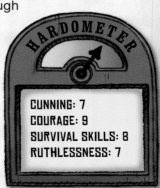

HARDOMETER

CUNNING: 7
COURAGE: 9
SURVIVAL SKILLS: 8
RUTHLESSNESS: 7

DEADLY DISEASES

Explorers had to be brave enough to go into unknown territory. They might find rough seas, arid deserts, freezing temperatures, or dangerous animals. But that wasn't all—deadly diseases were out to get them, too . . .

SCURVY

Scurvy has an unpleasant list of symptoms: aches and pains; tiredness; pale, blotchy, and bruised skin; swollen limbs; spongy, bleeding gums and loose teeth—and if it's left untreated, it's deadly. Scurvy is caused by a lack of vitamin C, which is found in fresh fruit and vegetables. In the 1740s, British navy doctor James Lind proved that eating lemons and limes could cure scurvy. Captain Cook (see page 20) gave his crew pickled cabbage to ward off the disease. However, doctors became convinced that scurvy was caused by something else. The disease plagued polar expeditions, such as Robert Scott's (see page 52), into the 1900s.

MALARIA

Malaria is caused by a tiny parasite that gets into the bloodstream through a mosquito bite. Since there are a lot of malaria-carrying mosquitoes, especially in Africa, explorers were often exposed to this horrible disease (David Livingstone, Richard Burton, and John Speke all suffered from it—see pages 34 and 26). Malaria sufferers experience flu-like symptoms, as well as diarrhea and vomiting, and the disease can kill. Malaria isn't the only deadly disease caused by mosquitoes, either. They can also carry yellow fever and dengue fever.

GANGRENE

In the days before antibiotics (which weren't discovered until the 1900s), infected wounds were very difficult to treat, and bad infections could lead to gangrene. If gangrene sets in, the skin turns dark green or black, the flesh starts to rot, and the wound stinks. If the injured part of the body isn't amputated, the sufferer can die.

As well as these deadly diseases, explorers suffered from all kinds of other horrible conditions caused by bad food, dirty water, freezing temperatures, and many types of germs.

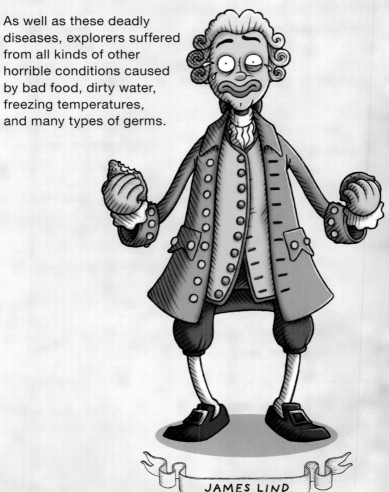

JAMES LIND

DAVID LIVINGSTONE

HARD AS NAILS RATING: 7.5

**David Livingstone was
a doctor and a missionary
who explored Africa. He ended up
leaving his heart there.**

LIVINGSTONE'S MISSION

David Livingstone was born in 1813 into a fairly poor
Scottish family. He started working in the local mill at the
age of ten. He saved money, went to university to study
medicine, and became a missionary—someone who goes
to foreign countries hoping to convert people
to Christianity.

MISSION IMPOSSIBLE

In 1840, Livingstone arrived at his post at the edge of the
Kalahari Desert in southern Africa. But he quickly became
more interested in exploring than in converting people
to Christianity—in fact, it's believed he only managed
to convert *one* person the whole time he was there! He
explored the region around the Zambezi River, searched
for the source of the Nile (like Burton and Speke, see
page 26), named Victoria Falls on the Zambezi, and
became the first European to cross
southern Africa. While he was
busy exploring, Livingstone used
his medical knowledge to help
people. He was especially good
at treating malaria, a disease
that still kills millions of people
today. He also campaigned
against slavery, which was
illegal in Britain but was still
common in Africa.

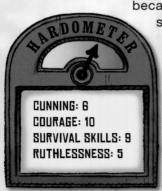

HARDOMETER

CUNNING: 6
COURAGE: 10
SURVIVAL SKILLS: 9
RUTHLESSNESS: 5

LOOKING FOR LIVINGSTONE

In Britain, Livingstone had become a celebrity, but he only returned twice. When there was no word from him for years, everyone wondered what had happened to him. An American newspaper sent journalist Henry Stanley to find him. It took Stanley eight months, but he found Livingstone living in a remote African village. He greeted him with the famous words "Dr. Livingstone, I presume?" and gave him all the letters that had been piling up for him while no one knew where he was.

LIVINGSTONE'S LAST JOURNEY

Livingstone stayed in Africa. When he died in 1873, his African friends dried out his body and carried it 930 miles (1,500 km) to the coast, where it was shipped to England and buried in Westminster Abbey. But his heart was buried in Africa.

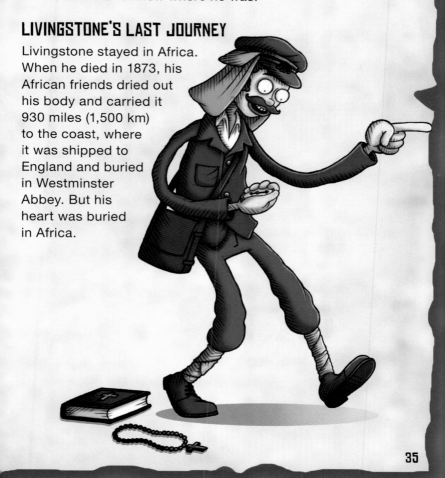

FERDINAND MAGELLAN

Ferdinand Magellan was a Portuguese explorer who led the first expedition to sail around the world.

EXPLORING AND CONQUERING

Ferdinand Magellan was 12 years old when Christopher Columbus (see page 10) discovered the New World on the other side of the Atlantic. He went to sea with the Portuguese fleet, which sailed east and conquered Malacca (in what is now Malaysia), and explored the Spice Islands, in what is now Indonesia. He was also the first European to see the Magellanic penguin!

WESTWARD EXPEDITION

Magellan proposed an expedition to find a westward route to the Spice Islands. The king of Portugal refused to fund it, so Magellan stormed off to Spain in anger. The Spanish king Charles I gave him five ships for his expedition.

In 1519, Magellan set sail across the Atlantic Ocean with a crew of around 250 men, hoping to find a route through Brazil to the Pacific Ocean. He didn't find one, because no such route existed.

MUTINY AND SHIPWRECK!

Some of the sailors were fed up with Magellan's expedition, so they mutinied. Magellan restored order by executing or marooning some of the men, but two ships were lost. One was wrecked on a reef, and another mutinied and escaped to Spain. Magellan carried on with the business of sailing around the world. He found a passage west around the tip of South America, sailing in rough seas past snow-capped mountains and the archipelago of Tierra del Fuego.

FATAL FIGHT

Since he was the first European ever to cross the Pacific Ocean, Magellan had no idea that it was so big. The expedition spent months without sighting land. With few provisions and hardly any fresh food, many of the crew members died of starvation or scurvy. But they eventually found the islands now called the Philippines. Unfortunately, Magellan didn't make himself very popular with the Philippine islanders. There was a battle during which Magellan was attacked by islanders and hacked to pieces.

THE EXPEDITION CONTINUES

Magellan was dead, but the expedition wasn't over. Two of the ships eventually returned to Spain, having successfully become the first ever to sail around the world.

HARDOMETER

CUNNING: 8
COURAGE: 9
SURVIVAL SKILLS: 6
RUTHLESSNESS: 10

MARCO POLO

Marco Polo was an Italian explorer who gave medieval Europe its first taste of Asia.

A LONG JOURNEY

Marco Polo's father and uncle were jewel merchants from Venice. They traveled all the way to China to trade their precious gems. When Marco Polo was 17, he went with them on a trip to China, sailing across the Mediterranean to Acre (now in Israel), then traveling by land across Asia to Shangdu—the court of the Mongol ruler of China, Kublai Khan. The journey took three and a half years.

THE COURT OF KUBLAI KHAN

Kublai Khan, Genghis Khan's grandson and ruler of the second-largest empire in the history of the world, was very impressed with Marco Polo. He was so impressed that he made him a diplomat, then governor of the city of Yangzhou. After 17 years at Kublai Khan's court, the Polos decided it was time to go home, but the emperor was very reluctant to let them leave.

HEADING HOME

In 1292, Marco Polo and his father and uncle set sail from southern China and began their journey home. Kublai Khan had asked them to escort a Mongol princess to Persia (modern-day Iran). After they dropped her off, they sailed to Constantinople (modern-day Istanbul), then traveled overland back to Venice. They had been away for 24 years.

THE TRAVELS OF MARCO POLO

In 1299, Marco Polo became a prisoner of war in Genoa. He told the story of his travels to a fellow prisoner, a writer called Rustichello, who wrote it all down. The book, which became known as *The Travels of Marco Polo*, included fantastic descriptions of Kublai Khan's palace (covered in gold and silver and big enough to hold 6,000 people for dinner), and Chinese inventions such as gunpowder, paper money, silk, and porcelain. Polo's adventures in China became famous and inspired other explorers, including Christopher Columbus. Marco Polo and his father and uncle never returned to China.

HARDOMETER

CUNNING: 8
COURAGE: 8
SURVIVAL SKILLS: 8
RUTHLESSNESS: 7

MUNGO PARK

Mungo Park was a Scottish doctor who explored western Africa—and disappeared there.

HARD AS NAILS RATING: 6

INTERIOR AFRICA

Mungo Park trained as a doctor but he wanted to be an explorer. He met a famous botanist named Joseph Banks, who had traveled with Captain Cook (see page 20) and was president of the Association for Promoting the Discovery of the Interior Parts of Africa—exactly what Park was interested in. In 1795, the association sent Park to western Africa to explore the Niger River.

IMPRISONED IN AFRICA

At that time, the slave trade was still legal in Britain, and Park's companions on the trip included Johnson, an ex-slave, and Demba, a slave who had been promised his freedom after the expedition. Park wore unsuitable European clothes for exploring, and kept his notes under his tall hat. Curious Bondou people made him hand over his umbrella and his coat, but far worse was to come. Park was taken prisoner by the emir of Ludamar, and poor Demba was taken away and sold. After four months, Park managed to escape with the help of Johnson, and continued his expedition. Park reached the Niger and followed it for 75 miles (120 km) before making his way to the coast to return to England.

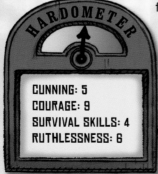

HARDOMETER

CUNNING: 5
COURAGE: 9
SURVIVAL SKILLS: 4
RUTHLESSNESS: 6

AFRICAN ADVENTURE

In 1805, Park began a second expedition to Africa with a team of around 40 people. But unwisely, they set off in the rainy season. Everyone in the team got sick, they were attacked by bandits, and the guide was nearly eaten by a crocodile. The expedition had left Portsmouth in January. When they reached the Niger in the middle of August, only 11 of them were still alive. Three months later, only five were left.

MYSTERIOUS DISAPPEARANCE

Park and his four companions set off down the Niger by canoe, but they never returned. Exactly what happened remains a mystery, but they were probably killed by hostile Africans. Park's body was never found. Over 20 years after his disappearance, his son Thomas went in search of his father. Sadly, he died of a fever before he got very far.

NEIL ARMSTRONG

Neil Armstrong's amazing journey into the unknown didn't take him across seas, mountains, deserts, or icy waters, but into outer space.

SPACE RACE

By the time Neil Armstrong was born in Ohio in 1930, most places on Earth had been explored. Space, on the other hand, was still a mystery. In 1961, Yuri Gagarin of the USSR became the first person to travel into space. After that, the USSR and the United States, the two biggest world powers at the time, raced each other to land people on the Moon.

ASTRONAUTS WANTED

Armstrong earned his pilot's license when he was just 16, then studied aeronautical engineering in university. His studies were interrupted by the Korean War, in which Armstrong flew fighter planes for the United States. Once he had finished his education, he went to work as a test pilot for NASA. He flew supersonic aircraft, as well as rockets, helicopters, and gliders. In 1962, he was chosen for the astronaut program—he was on his way to the Moon!

HARDOMETER

CUNNING: 8
COURAGE: 10
SURVIVAL SKILLS: 9
RUTHLESSNESS: 7

ONE SMALL STEP

The Apollo 11 mission blasted off on July 16, 1969. Three men made up the moon-bound team: Buzz Aldrin, Michael Collins, and the commander, Neil Armstrong. Just like explorers who lived hundreds of years before them, they were setting out into uncharted territory, with no back-up plan if things went wrong. On July 21, Armstrong landed the lunar module *Eagle*, and became the first person to set foot on the surface of the Moon, followed by Buzz Aldrin. They collected samples from the Moon's surface, and set up a mirror to help astronomers on Earth record the Moon's position.

MOON MAN

Armstrong instantly became one of the most famous people on Earth. His words when he was about to step onto the Moon— "One small step for a man, one giant leap for mankind"—became some of the most quoted ever. He never flew into space again, but he worked for NASA and as a professor of engineering. He passed away in 2012.

SPACE: THE FINAL FRONTIER

Neil Armstrong (see page 42) and his team are some of the most famous people who have ever been brave enough to travel into space. But there are other space pioneers too. . .

YURI GAGARIN

Yuri Gagarin, from the USSR (which is now Russia and other countries), became the first-ever person in space. In 1961, he orbited Earth in his spacecraft in just 89 minutes and 34 seconds.

VALENTINA TERESHKOVA

In 1963, Valentina Tereshkova (also from the USSR) became the first woman in space. The following year, she and her husband (who was also an astronaut) had a baby—the first person to be born whose parents had both traveled into space.

ALEXEI LEONOV

Alexei Leonov (from the USSR again) was the first person to spacewalk. In 1965, he left his spacecraft and stayed outside attached by a tether for over 12 minutes. His space suit had inflated while he was in space, and it was a tight fit for him to get back inside the spacecraft. Leonov had to open a valve in his suit to deflate it.

SPACE ANIMALS

The first creature from Earth in space wasn't human: fruit flies were sent up first! In 1957, Laika the dog became the first animal to orbit Earth. Other animals in space include tortoises, worms, monkeys, butterflies, bees, spiders, and jellyfish!

LIVING IN SPACE

Some people have lived on space stations for months on end, but living in space has its difficulties. Here are a few of them:

- Space sickness—just like any other kind of travel sickness—is a common problem.

- Astronauts have to be strapped into bed to go to sleep, and they have to get used to not having nighttime and daytime.

- Washing is a problem, because liquids form droplets that float away. So astronauts use soap that works without water.

- Zero gravity means that people don't use their muscles as much—they use exercise machines to stay in shape.

- Space food has to be lightweight and easy to store, so it's often freeze-dried, which isn't always very appetizing. And astronauts have to be careful not to make crumbs that can float off and clog up their instruments.

JUAN PONCE DE LEÓN

Spanish explorer Juan Ponce de León searched for the Fountain of Youth, founded the first colonial settlement in Puerto Rico, and was the first explorer to find Florida.

GOVERNING HISPANIOLA

We don't know for sure, but Juan Ponce de León might have begun his exploring career as part of Columbus's second expedition to the New World in 1493. We do know that by 1502 Ponce de León was a captain in the West Indies, working for the governor of Hispaniola (the second biggest island in the West Indies, now divided into Haiti and the Dominican Republic). Ponce de León ruthlessly put a stop to a mutiny by the local people, and was made governor of the eastern part of the island as a reward.

GOING FOR GOLD

Ponce de León wasn't just ruthless, he was greedy, too. He had heard reports of gold on the nearby island of Puerto Rico, so in 1508 he left to explore it. He founded Caparra, the oldest colonial settlement on the island, and became Puerto Rico's governor, until rivals kicked him out.

MAGIC FOUNTAIN

Ponce de León heard reports of a fountain of youth on an island called Bimini. Whoever drank from the fountain would become younger. He set off from Puerto Rico in 1513 and landed on the coast of Florida (which he named), close to the modern city of St. Augustine. He didn't realize he was on the edge of an enormous continent, instead of an island. He sailed south through the Florida Keys chain of islands, and landed farther south on Florida's coast, but he never found the magic fountain—which isn't all that surprising. No one's really sure whether Ponce de León really believed it existed.

CONQUERING

Ponce de León headed back to Spain, where he was made the governor of Florida and Bimini. Then he sailed all the way back to Florida again in 1521 to do more colonizing and conquering. But Ponce de León was stopped when hostile natives attacked, and wounded him with one of their arrows. He made it to Cuba, but died soon after.

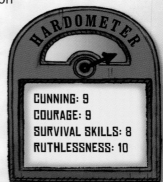

HARDOMETER

CUNNING: 9
COURAGE: 9
SURVIVAL SKILLS: 8
RUTHLESSNESS: 10

VASCO DA GAMA

Portuguese explorer Vasco da Gama sailed around the tip of Africa and opened a new sea route from Europe to the East.

HARD AS NAILS
RATING: 9

AROUND AFRICA

While Vasco da Gama was growing up, Portuguese explorers were sailing farther and farther down the western coast of Africa in search of a sea route to India. In 1488, Bartolomeu Dias reached the tip of Africa—the Cape of Good Hope—but didn't go any farther because his crew were too frightened of sea monsters and other dangers. King Manuel I of Portugal chose Vasco da Gama to sail around the Cape of Good Hope all the way to India.

EAST TO INDIA

In 1497, Vasco da Gama set sail from Lisbon with a fleet of four ships. He rounded the Cape of Good Hope and sailed across to India, arriving in Calicut (modern-day Kozhikode) in May 1498. The Hindu ruler was suspicious of the Europeans, but da Gama managed to load his ships with spices and jewels for his return trip to Portugal, which had to sail in the face of monsoon winds. When they finally arrived back in Portugal, two years after they had set out, only two of the ships were left, and just 55 of the 170 crew (many of them had died from scurvy).

HARDOMETER

CUNNING: 9
COURAGE: 9
SURVIVAL SKILLS: 9
RUTHLESSNESS: 9

SPICE ROUTE

Despite the losses, the king of Portugal was overjoyed with Vasco da Gama and rewarded him for his hard work. The new sea route could be used to trade in valuable eastern spices and jewels, and was a lot easier than lugging everything overland. This meant a huge money-making opportunity for Portugal. In 1502, da Gama set off on a second trip. He aimed to gain control of trade routes from the Arabs, and make everyone along the way swear loyalty to the king of Portugal. His methods were ruthless. One story says that he seized the cargo of a captured ship, then set fire to it with hundreds of passengers on board.

VICEROY OF INDIA

In the following years, Vasco da Gama's trade route made Portugal wealthy. In 1524, he was made viceroy of India, but he fell ill and died within a few months of arriving there.

MARY KINGSLEY

Mary Kingsley was a Victorian lady with a taste for adventure that took her all the way to Africa.

ADVENTURE CALLS

Mary Kingsley's father was a British doctor who traveled to the South Seas, the United States, and Africa. When he came home, he told stories of his adventures. Mary stayed at home and looked after her sick mother and her brother, but she yearned to travel. She had to wait until she was 30 before she could do anything about her plans. Both her parents had died, and they left enough money for Mary to live comfortably without having to work. But Mary didn't want to live comfortably—she wanted to go to Africa!

EXPLORING AFRICA

On her first African adventure, Kingsley sailed to the Canary Islands, then on to Sierra Leone and Angola, where she spent a few months living with local people and learning about African life. The following year, she went back. This time she visited the central African country of Gabon. She canoed up the Ogooué River and met the Fang people, who were said to be cannibals. She became an expert on African insects, and collected insects, fish, and plants for the British Museum as she traveled. She found several unrecorded species of fish, three of which were named after her. She also climbed the 13,123-foot-tall (4,000 m) Mount Cameroon—the first European woman to make the climb—via a route that no other European had attempted.

ALARMING TALES

When she got back to England, Kingsley wrote a book, *Travels in West Africa*, which became a bestseller. She also gave readings and lectures, that included many alarming stories. She spoke of how she drove away an attacking leopard by throwing a jug at it, and hit a crocodile on the head with her paddle as it tried to climb into her canoe. Kingsley returned to Africa in 1899 to work as a nurse in the Boer War, where she caught typhoid and died.

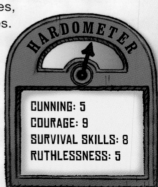

HARDOMETER

CUNNING: 5
COURAGE: 9
SURVIVAL SKILLS: 8
RUTHLESSNESS: 5

ROBERT FALCON SCOTT

Robert Falcon Scott led expeditions to one of the most perilous places on Earth—the freezing South Pole.

ANTARCTIC ADVENTURE

Robert Falcon Scott joined the British navy in 1871 when he was 13. Thirty years later, now an experienced sailor and a captain in the navy, he was chosen to lead an expedition to the Antarctic. He had never done any exploring before. But in 1901, he set off in command of the ship *Discovery*. The expedition lasted three years, and went farther south than anyone had before. The team returned to Britain as heroes.

ROALD WAS HERE

JOURNEY TO THE POLE

Despite the harsh conditions of the Antarctic, Scott was determined to return and be the first person to reach the South Pole. In 1911, he arrived on the frozen continent, leading a team of 12 men. Things began badly and only got worse. Many of the team's ponies died, and the dog teams turned back six months into the expedition, leaving five men to continue to the Pole. Scott and the others battled through terrible weather, dragging their own equipment with them. They finally reached the South Pole, only to find that Roald Amundsen (see page 8) and his team had beaten them to it by one month.

ICY DEATHS

Wearily, Scott and his small team began their 932-mile (1,500 km) journey back across the ice. The first person to die was a man named Evans—he fell into a crevasse and hit his head. Another member of the team, Oates, had frostbite, and sacrificed himself by walking out into the snow, rather than delay the others. Sadly, it made no difference: Scott and the remaining two men, Wilson and Bowers, died in their tent from starvation and exposure. They were only about 12 miles (19.3 km) away from supplies that might have saved them.

SNOWY TOMB

Eight months later, a search party found the bodies of the men and Scott's diary, which recorded their last journey. Scott, Wilson, and Bowers were buried under their tent, and their grave was marked by a snow memorial. In Britain, they were remembered as national heroes.

HARDOMETER

CUNNING: 5
COURAGE: 9
SURVIVAL SKILLS: 8
RUTHLESSNESS: 6

ZHENG HE

Zheng He traveled to Africa and India, expanding China's horizons farther than ever before.

SERVING THE PRINCE

Zheng He was born around 1371 in the mountainous Chinese province of Yunnan. When he was about 11, Yunnan was invaded by the mighty Ming dynasty, and Zheng He was captured and sent to serve Prince Zhu Di. Hostile northern groups were always attacking Prince Zhu Di's lands, and so Zheng He was constantly fighting them. He proved himself to be as hard as nails, and became one of the prince's chief advisers.

OVERTHROWING THE EMPEROR

Prince Zhu Di wanted to be emperor. When the old emperor died and Zhu Di's nephew took his place, he decided to do something about it. In 1402, with Zheng He as one of his chief commanders, he marched on the Chinese imperial capital and overthrew the emperor. Now that Zhu Di was the new emperor, Zheng He was promoted to a top job, and his exploring career could begin.

HARDOMETER

CUNNING: 8
COURAGE: 9
SURVIVAL SKILLS: 7
RUTHLESSNESS: 9

EXPLORING THE WORLD

Zheng He began the first of seven voyages in 1405. He set off in style, with maybe as many as 400 ships and more than 28,000 men. If that wasn't impressive enough, Zheng He himself was said to be more than 6.5 feet (2 m) tall, with a face as broad as a tiger's and eyebrows like swords—a man you wouldn't forget. His mission was to tell everyone how powerful and wonderful China was, as well as find out about the countries he visited, and make valuable trade routes. Altogether, he traveled around 31,000 miles (49,900 km). He visited India, Southeast Asia, Arabia, and East Africa, defeating pirates and anyone else brave enough to stand up to him. He brought back gifts of ivory, ostriches, zebras, and a giraffe, which the Chinese believed to be a mythical creature.

BURIED AT SEA

Zheng He probably died on his last voyage, in 1433. After his death, a new Ming emperor closed China to trade and even banned the building of seafaring ships. Zheng He was forgotten about for centuries, but now his fearless explorations are famous.

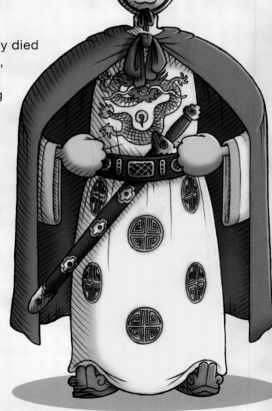

SIR WALTER RALEIGH

Walter Raleigh was an Elizabethan explorer who searched the New World for a fabled city of gold.

EXPLORING AMERICA

Raleigh was born around 1554 in England. He went to Oxford University and studied law in London. Then he got involved in British wars and revolts. But his first exploring experience came in 1578 when he sailed to America with his brother-in-law.

IRELAND, POTATOES, AND TOBACCO

Raleigh helped stop a rebellion in Ireland in 1580, making him one of Queen Elizabeth I's favorite young men. Later he helped defeat the Spanish armada, and she liked him even more. The queen made Raleigh captain of the guard, gave him plenty of land in Ireland, and he became a politician. But in the meantime, Raleigh went back to North America and tried (but failed) to found colonies. He is famous for bringing potatoes and tobacco back to Britain from his travels, but in fact the Spanish had already beaten him to it. He is probably responsible for making smoking popular, though. There is a story that someone threw a bucket of water over him thinking he was on fire, when in fact he was having a puff on his pipe.

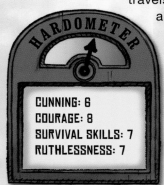

HARDOMETER

CUNNING: 6
COURAGE: 8
SURVIVAL SKILLS: 7
RUTHLESSNESS: 7

THE SEARCH FOR EL DORADO

In 1592, Raleigh got married. Queen Elizabeth was so upset that she threw Raleigh and his wife into the Tower of London. She didn't let them out until 1594. To try to get back into her good books, Raleigh set off on a voyage to find El Dorado—the fabled city of gold located somewhere in the New World. He traveled up the Orinoco River in South America, but didn't find the city.

EL DORADO AGAIN

When Queen Elizabeth died, King James I came into power. He didn't like Raleigh, and threw him into prison for 12 years. Then the king sent Raleigh to have another look for El Dorado, hoping to make Britain rich. When Raleigh didn't find the golden city, King James had him beheaded. Raleigh's wife kept his embalmed head in a bag until she died, when the head was finally buried.

HARD AS NAILS TRAVELERS AND EXPLORERS TIMELINE

970 CE

Leif Eriksson, the Viking explorer who sailed to North America, was born. He didn't stay in North America, but was probably the first European to ever go there.

1324

Marco Polo, who had traveled to China and was away from home for 24 years, died in Venice.

1405

Chinese explorer Zheng He set off on his first voyage. He traveled to Asia, Africa, the Middle East, and India.

1492

Christopher Columbus made his first voyage across the Atlantic to the West Indies.

1497

Vasco da Gama set sail on his journey around Africa to India, opening up a new trade route for Portugal.

1519

Ferdinand Magellan set off on the first ever round-the-world trip. He was killed in the Philippines before his ships completed the voyage.

1521

Juan Ponce de León, the first European to explore Florida, died. He tried and failed to find the Fountain of Youth.

1547

Hernán Cortés died, having conquered and ruled the Aztec Empire in the New World.

1618

Sir Walter Raleigh, English explorer of the New World, was executed. He searched for El Dorado, the legendary city of gold.

1768

Captain James Cook began his first voyage of exploration, which took him across all the world's oceans.

1795

Mungo Park set off to explore the Niger River in western Africa on his first expedition.

1803

Meriwether Lewis and William Clark set off on their journey from St. Louis in America's Midwest to the Pacific Ocean. They arrived home more than two years later.

1813

Explorer David Livingstone was born. He lived and worked in Africa for years, and later died there.

1857

Richard Burton and John Speke began their expedition to find the source of the White Nile.

1860

Robert Burke and William Wills set off on their trip across Australia. They made it from the south to the north of the continent, but died before they could make the return journey.

1872

Polar explorer Roald Amundsen was born. His expedition was the first to arrive at the South Pole, beating Robert Scott by about a month.

1893

Mary Kingsley made her first trip to Africa. She went on to climb Mount Cameroon, canoe up the Ogooué River, and become an expert on African insects.

1912

Robert Falcon Scott died on his expedition to the South Pole.

1937

Amelia Earhart went missing on her pioneering round-the-world flight. She was the first woman to cross the Atlantic by plane.

1969

Neil Armstrong became the first person to set foot on the Moon.

LEARNING MORE

BOOKS

Cummins, Julia. *Women Explorers*. Dial, 2012.

Gifford, Clive. *10 Explorers Who Changed the World*. Kingfisher, 2008.

Krull, Kathleen. *Lives of the Explorers*. HMH Books for Young Readers, 2014.

EDUCATIONAL WEBSITES

Famous Explorers, Bio: **www.biography.com/people/groups/famous-explorers**

Famous Explorers: **www.famous-explorers.org**

Women Explorers, National Geographic: **www.nationalgeographic.com/125/timelines/women-explorers**

GLOSSARY

ANTIBIOTICS Medicines that kill bacterial infections

AVIATOR The pilot of an aircraft

BESIEGED Surrounded by enemy forces

BOTANISTS Experts in plants

CIRCUMNAVIGATED Traveled all the way around something

COLONISTS People from another country who move into a new country and settle there

CONVENTION A way of behaving accepted and practiced in a particular society

CREVASSE A deep, open crack in a glacier or ice sheet

EMBALMED Treated a dead body with chemicals to preserve it

EMPIRE A group of states or countries ruled by one leader or state

ENSLAVING Forcing people to become slaves

EXPANSES Wide, open areas

GANGRENE The rotting of body tissue when wounds get infected

INFESTED Overrun with

MALARIA A deadly disease carried by mosquitoes

MAROONING Abandoning on a deserted island

MONSOON Strong winds that change direction each season

MUTINY A rebellion against authority

NOMADS People who move from place to place

NOTORIOUS Famous for something bad

ORBITED To go around an object in space

OUTLAW A criminal who is on the run from the law

REBELLION Break away from, or resistance to, authority

SCURVY A deadly disease caused by a lack of vitamin C

SUPERSONIC Faster than the speed of sound

TEEMING Full of

TYPHOID A deadly disease of the digestive system

VICEROY Governor representing the king or queen in a colony

INDEX